Grateful acknowledgements to the publications where these poems first appeared: *The Bastille* ("Me and Peggy Lee" and "Period."); *Redshift* ("Civilization" and "In the Dirt and Dead Leaves"); and *Small Fish Big Pond* ("Civilization," "Dead Cat," "Earliest Memory," "International Women's Day," and "When to Cry").

www.pictureshowpress.net

Cover image: iolya, istockphoto.com

FIRST EDITION

ISBN-13: 978-1-7324144-9-5
ISBN-10: 1-7324144-9-1

If your body is a broken landscape

Kathryn McMurray

Picture Show Press

POEMS

Your Last Chance

This is my last cigarette, my last beer, the last call
for help from the fluorescent lit hallway of the city jail.
This is my last piece of pizza, my last lap,
my last, best ex-boyfriend.
This is our last gig on the tour, the first song on our last album,
the last dance.
This is a picture of my last day of grade school, a picture
of the last time I saw you.
This is the last time I'm going to tell you;
eat your broccoli.
never call here again.
I love you.

About last night...
It was the last night we'll have together. It's all we've got
for the rest of our lives.
This is the last time I'll ever ask *you* for help again.
This is the last paycheck.
This is the last hair on the top of your head.
The last time you'll fit your foot into a size three.
The last sundown at 8pm.

These are the last stars of the evening.
These are the last rays of the sun, the sky is ever darkening
into night.
This is our last day in Eden. Let's eat and be naked
and roll around in the tall grass.
This is the last of its kind, a species in extinction, almost gone.
This is your last chance.

Red Lips

Her Candy Apple streaks slide into a pucker along soft pink wads
which grow to smacking bubbles, the pop, a starting gun
for ponytail giggles. The shade traded in the girls' bathroom
behind the gym, forgotten in a sweater pocket, rolled onto the
    jalopy floor,
then kept as a secret keepsake through the war. Later, her lips press
the glass edge, brush the cocktail napkin, smudge a uniformed collar,
leave the ghost of a kiss on cheek. Diablo Rosso Corsa raced across
a contrived pout and finished on the necks of lovers. Burgundy sip-
    worthy
mouth opens to a smirk. She was wearing Coquelicot when he knocked
on her father's door, Garnet when she got the ring.
A Cardinal grin on wedding day, radiating through thrown rice.
The return from the hospital caught her Amaranth kiss
in a photograph flash, lip print on soft new hair.
After that, a string of 4:45pm shades, lips in procession:
Coral, Berry, Blush, Terra Cotta, Firebrick.
Lacey evening serving aprons, Framboise stretched wide
across neat white teeth, a chilly martini waiting in the foyer.
In exchange for a sports coat, there's casseroles and Currant,
pot roast and Ruby, fricassee and Rosewood.
There were decades of demure drugstore pinks, hastily applied
in rearview mirrors, during carpool, in the grocery store parking lot.
Doing laundry, she spotted a strange Magenta on his collar,
hotel receipts in his pockets, a Merlot kiss and phone number scrawled
in a matchbook which spilled from a golf polo. It was Claret
when she found him slumped in the study, his Scotch still sweaty.
It was Vermillion when they buried him, handed her the flag.
A sigh escaped her Carnelian parted mouth, top teeth biting
    bottom skin.
The foul moan from her Sangría scowl is just the result of a dull,
    constant headache.
In the end, there's Chapstick. She brings a reptilian tongue to the waxy
smoothness, and she remembers the blush of bubble gum.

Leaping

To the dead cat in the road

I saw you, eyes and dried blood and fur, out in the street,
right there, splayed across the middle and right lanes.
Your body, a bump before a stop light.
Like everyone else, I passed by,
on my way, a mundane destination pulling
me through the morning traffic.
Maybe they winced too, the other drivers,
or maybe not. No one stopped.
Still in my rear view, I looked again.

Dead cat in the road, for a moment,
I saw with your eyes, the lane lines past my muzzle.
I sniffed the air and thought, *there's a gap to shoot through.*
The hot tar beneath my pads, old gas floating up
from the summer street steam, across the road
a nice hedge for hiding. This, as good a time as any
to dart out, risk crossing. My legs are strong. Damn the traffic.
Here is my double-dutch second. Here is my chance.

I took the leap, now watch me go.

Ward 4, Community Hospital of Long Beach

Three smoke breaks, and you take them
even if you don't smoke.
Slippers, shoes strangled by rubber bands, socks pinched
into flip flops, we scuff the dirty linoleum to the line.
Some lean on dirty walls, others cough,
a few make conversation as if coworkers,
or customers in line at the bank, talking about
how they slept, how they can't wait to get some air.

We are in various states of cleanliness. Some care. Some don't.
Antonio, a tattooed old Picasso in a hospital gown,
doesn't even know what's happening.
He paces the hallway over and over,
and we are reminded why we're here.

There are unexplained injuries, scabs, casts, and a black eye
or two, but we all shuffle forward to a big young man,
half-smirking, who hands us free cigarettes, one at a time,
then walks to the door and nods to buzz us through.
It's a crazy buzz, the kind you expect from movies
like *One Flew Over the Cuckoo's Nest*. There's even a Ratchett
behind the glass frowning, chasing us down for meds every few hours.

After the buzz, we do the loony dash, more like a hobble,
to get out to the patio, feel the air.
Like half-dead grass, the patients lean toward the sunlight
through the chain link morning, because inside
it's all smeared and tagged plexiglass, fog-like barrier
to the panorama of Long Beach, a rarified view.

You get 15 minutes for the day. And no one talks,
unless they're *really* crazy.
There is pacing, rocking, mumbling.
The ones who can't hold their own cig are helped.

The air, up so high on the 13th floor, is cold but good.
That sunlight feels like a gift.
There's quiet and wind.
There's the sound of mouths exhaling smoke.
There's the sound of the rest of the world waking,
starting cars, going to work.
It's a bit of wire-restricted freedom. We are grateful. We savor it.
Someone says, "The sun feels good."
This is the truth, so we grunt gently in agreement.

What 1970's Television Taught Me about Women

For Joan Jobe Smith

Women can fight crime and bring justice to the downtrodden
if they are Caucasian, over six feet tall, have long, flowing locks
(impossibly blonde or deeply brunette),
wear tight bell bottoms, have bionic body parts, know karate, can
shoot semi-automatic weapons,
accurately speak numerous foreign languages, own a magic lasso
and bullet-deflecting bracelets,
and know how to drive a custom Lotus at top speeds while being
chased down narrow streets
in either San Francisco or Bangkok by either minions of an evil
genius or ninjas on motorbikes.

However, women who fight crime and bring justice to the
      downtrodden
must be single, obtusely focused on fighting evil, and somewhat
resistant to sexual advances,
flirty but frigid to most men, unless, *unless* he is:
      a superhero with superior powers,
      another superhero equal in power, though the affair will
            only last for an episode or two,
      a lowly comic figure, a generic lab scientist, tech nerd, or
      hack journalist, who will only receive attentions for
      a single scene or, if lucky, one episode, or
      an evil, but powerful figure, who seduces through gifts and
      promises, which will ultimately be
            taken away at the last minute,
            turned into a bomb, or similar device which threatens to
            destroy the world, or
            cannot be fulfilled because said evil genius cannot resist
            the lures and temptations of evil and vice, in comparison
            with the smallish rewards of morality and sincerity.

If a woman who fights crime and brings justice to the downtrodden
    accepts a mission,
from the CIA, FBI, DMA, DOD, SIS, MI anonymous special
    operatives, or the Universe,
she must complete her mission successfully; otherwise, her show
    will be canceled.
If she completes too many missions successfully, with evildoers
    incarcerated
and bad guys ruined too frequently, her show will be canceled. As a result,
the last episode includes a black frame stating,
To be continued...

Moon Travel

In zero gravity, a bra floats past a console of bleeps and bloops.
No one is wondering if NASA's soap dries out the complexion,
but how *do* you change a tampon in a space suit?

38,000 miles away from Earth, the lunar pull is familiar.
A great, great, great grandmother of mine must have stared up
at the same moon from a prairie in Missouri 160 years ago.

I see her doubled over, clothespin in hand. Her face a grimace.
Sanitary belt pinching her waist, she digs a boot into the soil,
the Earth, straightens her back and then continues her work.

Linens collected, she pauses to breathe and, head tilted up
to the sky, there she sees the moon in day, white and full,
gazing back at her with sympathy, pulling her home.

That night, the cramps throb. She turns and tosses
in the moonlight beaming in through her window,
splayed over her abdomen,
but once sleep comes,
she dreams of stars, the dusty surface of strange places,
dark and open silence,
and laughing, naked women floating,
spinning through a void.

Me and Peggy Lee

When she first showed up, I was fifteen.
Drunk on Sprite and box rosé, I wanted Peter Rascoe to kiss me,
but he didn't. So, I stumbled through the kids smoking
pot in the cream carpet hallway, knocked a picture of a smiling family
off the wall as I did, tried one doorknob and then another,
electric blue mascara streaming down my face with each try,
my ponytail coming loose (I had lost one of my cupcake earrings.
Where was it?), and finally a bathroom door opened.
Spinning, I wheeled around to slam it shut, and when I turned,
there she was, sitting in the bathtub wearing a pink sequined gown.
A long cigarette holder and martini in one hand,
she adjusted her white fur shrug with the other.
Patting the toilet seat cover, she exhaled smoke that said,
"Sit down, little sister." And I did. I listened to her
lazy drawl asking *Is that all there is?* while I puked my guts out.

After that, I saw her from time to time.
She crashed my high school graduation, crooned at me
in the student lounge during my college years,
danced with my Uncle Dave at our wedding
while her entourage, a German oompah band
in seersucker suits and straw banded hats, forlornly wailed.
I begged her to stop, but she didn't.
She held my son's umbilical cord, blowing smoke in the doc's
face, as she muttered through teeth clenching a cigarette holder,
"What a dame. What a dame."

Fed up with me and Peggy Lee, I swore I'd kill her. And I did it.
Now, I know what you're asking yourself,
"How'd you do it? How'd you end it all?" And I'll tell you.
 When I was thirty six years old, I had a nervous breakdown.
I planned it that way. I poured her a drink and set out an ashtray.
Her favorite scent is Despair. I bathed myself in it.
I stripped down, climbed in the tub and waited.

As I closed my eyes, I felt a ripple in the water
and suddenly there she was, dripping wet and sitting
at the opposite end of the tub. The fall of platinum ringlets on her head
drooped wet, her false eyelashes cocked and eyeliner crooked,
and that damned pink sequined gown soaked through
so that I could see her falsies. She lit a cigarette and smirked.
"What gives, little sister?"

I want to say it was easy, but it wasn't.
A fair amount of Despair spilled from the tub.
Bubbles from her leer beneath the surface, a thrash,
a sputter. I swear she cackled under water.
The ashtray was smashed and she bloodied my face
with her champagne talons, but I shoved her head under
until she was gone. On the water's surface floated
her broken cigarette holder and those platinum ringlets.
That was all there was left of Peggy Lee.

The After Bath

After "What I Saw in the Water" (1938) Frida Kahlo

The bath water gathers sloughed skin—
the grime, the oils, slivers of cells, traces of the day—
mingles all this in the glassy, silent brew,
then produces the steam of you, of personal memory,
of public history,
all swirling and settling, wafting about your face.
But you are dumb, transfixed by the heat and the stillness,
confronted by the mass of jagged images floating in the tub—
your loves, wars and wounds, conflagrations and births—
an active still life—
until you pull the plug.

Period.

Over and out.
My days of birthing babies are over.
I close the ovarian curtains, take a bow.
I left one to the ether, then labored over two.
In this bloody show, there's no more take,
no profit to collect for the work.
I can see now why they call it *the curse*;
the blood hangs on, though I'm done
with childbirth. Every twenty-eight days I twist
and ache (Too hysterical? Too much?), and for what?
Wax and wane? Chain myself to some old moon?
I'm still young enough to screw,
but too old to pursue it; weary of dates,
wary of sexual wiles,
bloated.

My uterus: a weak votive candle to old Fertility.
If I wanted, there's a goddess, a saint, I could pray to.
I could demand *Give me life, growth in this womb!*
But I don't. I won't. Instead, I bleed and bleed;
this empty sanguine ritual pesters me
like a be-laced old Catholic grandmother,
you still have time... still have time... still have time.
I'm done. Do you hear me, old mother?
Here's what I want to do: destroy, smash and burn
that old clock. Hear me? With your ticking and tocking,
I'm done.
Full stop.

Taper in the Dark

To be, or not be; a poignant question at the age of 21,
sitting in a community college classroom, pregnant
with my first love's baby. Ophelia didn't seem so mad.
Filling pockets with rocks and dropping down to the murky
    depths...
now *there's* an idea. I'd leave class and return to the little room
we shared in your mother's house, where we'd made this baby,
where we tumbled and tugged and panted, even while it grew.
I cried after, and you didn't know what to do with me.
She tried to talk me out of it, your mother, but then I'd turn to your face,
try to see down the road through your eyes, tried to imagine age there,
and I couldn't. I couldn't. I couldn't.
Getting sick, morning after morning, in the shit-lined toilet
of the vintage store that I worked in, helped me understand lost love.
I'll do what you want to do wasn't much relief.
You laid the decision at my heart, a damned spot that wouldn't rub out.

That blood spot, it kept coming and coming, not just then, but now even.
When I got pregnant again, this time married, an honest woman,
the repeated history—*Is this your first pregnancy?*—haunted me.
I waddled and swayed through the halls during grad school,
and eased my swollen belly into those small desks, feeling my son
kick my intestines while I read *Macbeth* and *Othello*.
What's done will never be undone; *only I had to live with that,*
and be reminded at each sonogram and check-up, hearing his heart
beating, beating to tell about the serpent beneath the flower.

You, father to that drowned baby, that indecisive madness,
haven't lived with Shakespeare like that. I see you from time to time,
once while you were on a date, just after my son was born.
I hid and watched you with your girl. She seemed about 21. Young.
You were going to the movies; you put your hand on the small of
    her back.
I wondered about that hand. *Will these hands ne'er be clean?*

Did you ever think of them as unclean? Is there a taper in the dark
that follows you into your dreams, sleepwalking its way into your plans,
flickering at you whenever you come? You went down the stair;
I felt my milk and left you there.

Other People

In some remote cabin
tucked into a snow-capped mountain,
there's another me
who has gotten what she always wanted:
silence, good books,
warm clothes for winter,
dresses and sandals for summer,
wandering brooks, hikes, solitude,
sunshine, a little music to dance to,
a crackling fire and the smell of plants everywhere.
Freedom.

In this other life, I tell myself I like the quiet,
that the abstract serenity has become concrete.
Some days, though, I just don't feel like chopping firewood,
and the percolator makes an annoying gargle sound.
I find that I miss arguing about nothing.
When I've read *Walden* for the tenth time,
I am suspicious of Thoreau.

But then you'd come traipsing up the mountain
and I'd miss the wind again.
You'd pick up my book and ask me what it was about.
I'd hear your breathing in the night
and fall in love with the percolator instead.
Suddenly, chopping wood is my favorite pastime,
and goddammit Thoreau.

In the Dirt and Dead Leaves

My cat Lola is dragging her hind legs across the back porch.
Her legs are limp, and she strains against her own weight,
pulling herself little by little across the concrete.
Because she can no longer clean herself properly,
her grey calico fur is matted all along her back.
She wants to be alone in the dirt and dead leaves.

Twenty years ago, she fit in the palm of my hand.
She liked to nap inside my dirty running shoes back then.
No matter how many overpriced pet beds I brought home,
Lola always curled up in the dirt, in the dust, in the dark.
She did not grow into a loving or pretty cat.
We had to warn visitors not to pet.

I got the feeling that Lola waited all day, every day,
to escape, and she took every chance she got.
When she got out, I spent hours calling,
in the night or in the day, down alleys, yelling into crawl spaces,
leaving open cans of food at the back door,
cooing "Here Kitty, Kitty!" into the moldy darkness
beneath the apartment building.
Sometimes she'd be gone for days.
She never came back willingly. I pulled her,
hissing, yowling, by the paws, by the tail
out of the grime, covered in cobwebs, eyes wild.

When I pick her up, she is light and she doesn't fight.
Her legs dangle uselessly, no kicking or scratching.
She doesn't make a noise. She closes and opens her eyes.
Across the patio is a cushion, a bowl of water, food.
I set her down. I move slow, gentle.
On her cushion, I stroke above her nose.
But now she's moving, dragging herself away again.
She's using all the energy she's got.
Maybe for the last time, maybe not.
She's headed for the dirt and the dead leaves.

Like Leaves, We Dull in Winter

Deep sepia tresses become braided in silver strands.
Goldenrod mops blow, grazing the face, gradually
turning to faded flaxen. Complexions fade,
from fresh peach to ashen, pallid expressions of doubt, dismay.
Why the long face? Is the dulling too much to take?

A fact: life culminates, and then recedes;
You didn't enjoy the peak? The technicolor wonder
of fifteen? You didn't embrace the luminosity of nineteen?
Or the fault, ruin, successes of the prismatic world of twenty?
What about the dissonance of color compounds in your thirties?
You are losing ground now... we approach forty.

I found my first grey at thirty-five—
alive enough to still drink heavily, orgasm readily,
and rebel unrepentantly. I am not an old, old woman,
but I am older than my former self.
Looking in the mirror,
I discovered cinereal brink of age.
I was catapulted to my death, burial, burning...
The ashiness of my teenage longing, the burnt offering
of my young adult hoping, the scalded, smoking
campfire remnants of adult goals. There's a fire,
but it's almost put out. The stink of slate smoke remembers,
lingers, in a desperate thrall of flame: indigo licking a titian bowel
of violet encrusted pain. Bluntly, youth burns out, and quickly.

Who laments but the middle-aged? Kids, tweens, hot-assed
teens posting nasty pictures on Snapchat, twenty-one year olds
criticizing forbears, be forewarned.

Age comes when you least expect it.
Disbelieve, if you will, until you yourself, find silver

slithering down your scalp. The silver knell will happen, and how
then will you reckon your life and deeds? Think, think: we all
concede. Silver-gilded hair will get you. Nothing will impede.
Nothing, nothing, but death, which is always approaching.
You will die, young thing. It's a fact. Life culminates, then recedes.

Survival of the Fittest

There was a Neanderthal woman
who just didn't feel like crushing berries.
Maybe she had a toothache.
Maybe she just felt like laying around.
The weather was pretty nice this time of year, so why rush?

There was a Pictish lady
who just couldn't get into
skinning another rabbit.
I mean, she loved rabbit,
but she just felt like dangling
her fingers in a nice cold stream.
It had been a long, lovely spring... so why rush?

There was this peasant woman in a French village.
Even though the King was passing through the streets,
throwing gold coins into the air,
and doing scrofula all over the lepers,
she kind of liked how quiet it
got with everyone in town.
She just felt like curling up
and taking a little snooze
while everyone gawked at the King.

My great grandmother stared at the dusty porch,
then out across the field, broom in hand.
Every one of her ten children had left a footprint.
And there was bread to make and clothes to wash.
Still, she wondered if that old tire swing still hung
on the oak tree by the creek, and if it'd hold her weight.

And there was that time my Nana could've met Elvis.
And that time my mom could've finished high school.

I wake up early on Saturday,
knowing that I need to get in a run if I want to survive the Robot
    Zombie Apocalypse,
but I just want to scratch my butt and eat another bagel.

The Chill

Steam rose from his skin under the delivery room lights,
and then he was swaddled tight, passed to me carefully,
his pursed lips mouthing for my sweaty nipple.
When we came home that night, there were knit booties
and chenille blankets in wait. We hiked up the thermostat.

He's four now and I come home from work late, kiss his forehead,
hold his chilly, sleeping hand, and re-tuck that body
into different blankets.
How much colder can he get?
His arms seem long, legs sprawled.

That night, during lecture, my students were suspicious and resistant.
I feel the contrast now, in my new son's room, by degrees.
He doesn't wake but groans and slips into the crook of my arm.
He sighs and shifts. The fall cold is seeping in.

My son is three months old. Done with feeding,
I leave him in his crib
for the porch, a sweater and a glass of wine, thinking of my husband's
grandmother dying. In the sharpness of moonlight, I remember
nothing could keep her warm. There were booties and shawls,
but memories still crept in. She was annoyed.
Fussing angered her. The nurses tried to spoon
her steaming soup and she spat it out.
She scratched them with her warped fingernails.
She allied herself with the chill. This is something I understand,
but wish I didn't. That's the truth, tell me, isn't it?

A Work in Progress

After "The Broken Column" (1944) by Frida Kahlo

If your body is a broken landscape, what empire has been toppled?
Braced ribs and breast become cracked column,
held together with blood and paint, an ode
to building up and tearing down for the sake of it.
A canvas toga drapes across ancient cactus deserts
where sandaled soldiers drag their drums and banners
yesterday and today.
The land, the body, the work—undone.
Always a work in progress.

When to Cry

When they are telling you to say your goodbyes,
when everyone else is gaunt and ghostly,
when all you can do is buy groceries,
and stare out windows at the effect of wind,
this is not the time to cry.

Even when you've said goodbye,
even when the moment has passed
and an official date to remember everything
with everyone has been set, even when
you put on a black dress and talk as if you
are saying real words, and even then...
it is not the time to cry.

In these moments, you may let appropriate tears out,
one drop at a time, let your throat burn
and swallow down clichés about grief,
which slide into your chest and stay, cold
and heavy and tight, right on top of your heart.

The time to cry comes without calling for it.
Months later, you are doing the dishes,
maybe waiting for the bus, folding laundry.
The sun is shining, and there's this song playing,
a song that makes you want to dance.
This is when you cry.

International Women's Day

My son comes home crying on International Women's Day.
His backpack is filled with crumpled pages and he takes them out,
evidence of unfairness, throwing them on the floor.
Susan B. Anthony's grim line of a mouth stares out
from these pages at third grade American boys and girls.
A cartoon of Marie Curie plays with beakers, hair swept up,
smock cinched tight, and Rosa Parks smirks through a mug shot.

But right now, my son is crying, red-faced, fighting my arms.
Why do women get a special day? He asks.
The girls in his class leered, they laughed, and lorded the day
over the boys in Room B207. Tayler's blond ponytail whipped
his sense of fairness, Emma's glitter ballerina slippers danced
on all those little quiet talks about equality in the dark
at bedtime, my voice down to a whisper, hope pulsing
in my throat as I brushed strands of hair from his little forehead
and promised him a new world. And he dreamt, trusting me.

In a third-grade way, I have to answer that question.
I know it won't be enough, but this is what I say,
I say, you came from a woman, all of us did.
And how you feel now? That unfair lump in your throat?
That's how it felt to be a woman for centuries, thousands of years
of swallowing dreams hard, digesting and reformulating a face for
        this world.
It's a grim line of a mouth that every woman wears.
Because you come from me, it's in you too.
You're choking on that lump, so it brings tears.

Breastfeeding Liam at 2 AM

At first he is cow-like, his pupils dilated in the dark,
eyes soft and round and black, still asleep, grazing at the nipple,
guided more by instinct than hunger. His pace is a country mosey.

But soon a storm crosses the horizon of his face.
His brow turns Cro-Magnon and Mars red,
arms jerk out and legs flail.
He's swimming in the air for his life.
He rears off the breast;
A horse startled by a gunshot;
A cough is followed by a raspy cry
and then his mouth tries to find its place again.
But it can't.
His head wobbles, mouth gaping open
like those desperate Koi fish at the Japanese gardens.

I'm worried he won't eat. I try to shove his face back to the breast.
The books say to do it this way.
But he resists me, and I'm surprised at his two-month old strength.
His tongue searches his own mouth for the nipple,
but he pushes his chin into the air away from me.
His back is arched
and my hand cups his entire head.
I can feel his scalp sliding over his skull.
It's a weird dance... one minute he lunges toward me,
and the next it's as though I've burned him.
I suddenly feel the fight between us, a struggle
that stretches long into the future.
I'm killing his will and I have to
for his own sake.
At 2am, today, it's breastfeeding.
And tomorrow?
I understand this is my first lesson in motherhood.
I am a force. He is a will.

Beast

A man sleeping after good sex is like a beast,
in the best sense, snoring sonorously, deeply
satisfied with himself and the world.
The zees escape him, each like the last exhale.
There are no ideas here. No plans. Just the deep
satisfactory dreaming of a body spent wisely.
He is full in the way he should be, needs to be.
His limbs lay limp and tingling in his dreaming,
telling him what to dream, speaking to him
of his body, not his job, not philosophy, not content,
rather content, a warm and slow filling of some emptiness,
so that the emptiness seems strange,
and fullness, a womanly thing, is familiar.

I Pray on the Dark Lord, Mommy

A small, dark storm enters the living room one afternoon,
when your not-quite-four-year-old son invokes the devil:
I pray on the Dark Lord, Mommy.
Mini lightning bolts shoot out in jagged strikes around his face.
A tiny thunderclap bounces off your recently polished hardwood floors.
His eyes are narrowed in a twisted-tike scowl,
knowing that Time Out will not begin to address this proclamation.

At this moment you pause, wondering if perhaps the Mötley Crüe
concert attended while pregnant could have germinated this seed.
You stare back, hard.
He responds with *I don't like God, Mommy,*
challenging you to defend the deity that you decried in your twenties
during furious drunken spoutings of liberal atheist bullshit.
He grips his Buzz Lightyear defiantly. Hardened. Stoic.
It is naptime he fears.

You steel yourself against his invocation and order him to bed,
not sure if he will comply and pad off in his small bare feet,
or if swarms of hissing demons will encircle you both,
sending the whole suburban abode up in flames,
bringing down the town, the county, the country.

A moment flickers between you, and you feel it pass.
For now, the Dark Lord's minion has decided that a nap
wouldn't be such a bad idea. You hear him slam the door
in derision, mocking you; for it is *his* choice, not yours.
But you let out a whoosh of air and grip your sides.
Today, we will not die.

Civilization

I was a beast child.
Feral rage-cry ripped my gut open,
unleashed by some deep old sister
lodged somewhere in my juvenile spine.
Do not come near, said my wild eyes.
I fought you off, you and your arms,
with tooth, nail, open-palm slap,
with fierce little pinch and hot spit.
I bent your ring finger back.

I don't know why I was mad now.
I was eight, maybe nine.
But it felt good to let it out—
that murder in my blood.
I had Cain's rock held over a head.
A foot on someone's throat.

But you trapped me in your arm,
a brutal scoop, a wrestling move that stilled
the fiend in me. Your fingers seemed to snap
shut, and no matter my twists and screams,
you held me fast, tight,
though I whipped my hair in your face,
cursed, sweat, vowed to run away
the second you let go.
But you didn't. You locked your grip.

Mother, how long did that gruff hug last?
How long did you hold your wild child
until she surrendered her burden?
How long did it take to make me a person?

Earliest Memory

I am watching a bearded man ride my red tricycle in the driveway
of a house that I can't even develop into a concrete image.
On the edge of a softly fraying mental picture, there is burnt sienna grass
and an airbrushed-van sunset. There is a black dog barking behind
    a neighbor's fence.
My mom and her friends are standing in cut-offs and sweatshirts,
    barefooted,
cigarettes in hand, all frozen in laughs of varying intensity.
They watch him boozily swoop around the concrete,
nearly tipping over as he rounds a corner.

Likely, there are details I have misremembered.
Still, I hold onto these facts:
My tricycle was red. The man's name was Gus. His beard was black
    and curly.
Burnt sienna is a Crayon color.
There was a black dog barking behind a neighbor's fence.

My mother has told me that some of this wrong.
She wanted to edit some characters in or out. She changed the location.
I scribble over these revisions with my burnt sienna Crayon.
There are several details about this event.
Did I misremember? Whose memory is it?
The tricycle was red. Gus had black hair. The neighbor had a mean dog.
She has tried to reconcile burning cigarettes and the red tricycle,
the toddler standing on the edge of an evening in the late 1970s.
There were no bare feet, she told me, no boozy laps.
It was the late 70s, but not an evening, she said.
The air-brushed van is an invention.

There are several details.
I don't know who belongs to the details:
Frozen laughs of varying intensity. Cut-off jean shorts. Red tricycle.
A black dog barking behind a neighbor's fence.

ACKNOWLEDGMENTS

This book wouldn't have been possible without the support and urging of a few loving people who know how lazy I am. First, I would like to thank editor extraordinaire Shannon Phillips for her belief in me and her willingness to nudge me continuously. Thank you to Suzanne Allen and *Small Fish, Big Pond* for always including me and pushing me along. Thank you to Charles Webb for an excellent education and good advice.

I would also like to thank my wonderful husband Shannon McMurray, who has been telling me that I need to put out a chapbook for many years. Thank you for always encouraging me, my love. Thank you to my sons, Liam and Jonah, for inspiring me and reminding me of what is always most important: love.

Thank you to Ayn, Anna, Jhoanna, Ja'net, Oceana, Jean, Jennifer and my creative and lovely mother Melanie.

www.ingramcontent.com/pod-product-compliance
Lightning Source LLC
Chambersburg PA
CBHW021148020426
42331CB00005B/962